SCHOLASTIC

C000229139

READ & RESPOND

Bringing the best books to life in the classroom

Activities based on **Kensuke's Kingdom** By Michael Morpurgo

Terms and conditions

IMPORTANT – PERMITTED USE AND WARNINGS – READ CAREFULLY BEFORE USING

Copyright in the software contained in this CD-ROM and in its accompanying material belongs to Scholastic Limited. All rights reserved. © 2015 Scholastic Ltd.

Save for these purposes, or as expressly authorised in the accompanying materials, the software may not be copied, reproduced, used, sold, licensed, transferred, exchanged, hired, or exported in whole or in part or in any manner or form without the prior written consent of Scholastic Ltd. Any such unauthorised use or activities are prohibited and may give rise to civil liabilities and criminal prosecutions.

The material contained on this CD-ROM may only be used in the context for which it was intended in *Read & Respond*, and is for use only by the purchaser or purchasing institution that has purchased the book and CD-ROM. Permission to download images is given for purchasers only and not for users from any lending service. Any further use of the material contravenes Scholastic Ltd's copyright and that of other rights holders.

This CD-ROM has been tested for viruses at all stages of its production. However, we recommend that you run virus-checking software on your computer systems at all times. Scholastic Ltd cannot accept any responsibility for any loss, disruption or damage to your data or your computer system that may occur as a result of using either the CD-ROM or the data held on it.

IF YOU ACCEPT THE ABOVE CONDITIONS YOU MAY PROCEED TO USE THE CD-ROM.

Recommended system requirements:
Windows: XP (Service Pack 3), Vista (Service Pack 2), Windows 7 or Windows 8 with 2.33GHz processor
Mac: OS 10.6 to 10.8 with Intel Core™ Duo processor
1GB RAM (recommended)
1024 x 768 Screen resolution
CD-ROM drive (24x speed recommended)
Adobe Reader (version 9 recommended for Mac users)
Broadband internet connections (for installation and updates)

For all technical support queries (including no CD drive), please phone Scholastic Customer Services on 0845 6039091.

Designed using Adobe Indesign
Published by Scholastic Ltd,
Book End, Range Road, Witney,
Oxfordshire OX29 0YD
www.scholastic.co.uk

Printed and bound by Ashford Colour Press
© 2015 Scholastic Ltd
1 2 3 4 5 6 7 8 9   5 6 7 8 9 0 1 2 3 4

British Library Cataloguing-in-Publication Data A catalogue record for this book is available from the British Library.
ISBN 978 1407 14224 1

Extracts from *The National Curriculum in England, English Programme of Study* © Crown Copyright. Reproduced under the terms of the Open Government Licence (OGL). http://www.nationalarchives.gov.uk/doc/open-government-licence/open-government-licence.htm

Due to the nature of the web, we cannot guarantee the content or links of any site mentioned. We strongly recommend that teachers check websites before using them in the classroom.

Author Jillian Powell
Editorial team Rachel Morgan, Jenny Wilcox, Jennie Clifford, Tracy Kewley
Series designer Neil Salt
Design team Ian Foulis and Mike Connor
Illustrator Gemma Hastilow
Digital development Hannah Barnett, Phil Crothers and MWA Technologies Private Ltd

Acknowledgements
The publishers gratefully acknowledge permission to reproduce the following copyright material:

Michael Foreman for the use of the cover and illustrations from *Kensuke's Kingdom* by Michael Morpurgo, illustrated by Michael Morpurgo. Illustrations © 1999, Michael Foreman (1999, Egmont UK Ltd).
David Higham Associates for the use of extracts from *Kensuke's Kingdom* by Michael Morpurgo. Text © 1999, Michael Morpurgo (1999, Egmont UK Ltd).

Every effort has been made to trace copyright holders for the works reproduced in this book, and the publishers apologise for any inadvertent omissions.

CONTENTS

▼ INTRODUCTION

Read & Respond provides teaching ideas related to a specific children's book. The series focuses on best-loved books and brings you ways to use them to engage your class and enthuse them about reading.

The book is divided into different sections:

- **About the book and author:** gives you some background information about the book and the author.

- **Guided reading:** breaks the book down into sections and gives notes for using it with guided reading groups. A bookmark has been provided on page 8 containing comprehension questions. The children can be directed to refer to these as they read.

- **Shared reading:** provides extracts from the children's books with associated notes for focused work. There is also one non-fiction extract that relates to the children's book.

- **Grammar, punctuation & spelling:** provides word-level work related to the children's book so you can teach grammar, punctuation and spelling in context.

- **Plot, character & setting:** contains activity ideas focussed on the plot, characters and the setting of the story.

- **Talk about it:** has speaking and listening activities related to the children's book. These activities may be based directly on the children's book or be broadly based on the themes and concepts of the story.

- **Get writing:** provides writing activities related to the children's book. These activities may be based directly on the children's book or be broadly based on the themes and concepts of the story.

- **Assessment:** short activities that will help you assess whether the children have understood concepts and curriculum objectives. They are designed to be informal activities to feed into your planning.

The activities follow the same format:

- **Objective:** the objective for the lesson. It will be based upon a curriculum objective, but will often be more specific to the focus being covered.

- **What you need:** a list of resources you need to teach the lesson, including digital resources (printable pages, interactive activities and media resources, see page 5).

- **What to do:** the activity notes.

- **Differentiation:** this is provided where specific and useful differentiation advice can be given to support and/or extend the learning in the activity. Differentiation by providing additional adult support has not been included as this will be at a teacher's discretion based upon specific children's needs and ability, as well as the availability of support.

The activities are numbered for reference within each section and should move through the text sequentially– so you can use them while you are reading the book. Once you have read the book, most of the activities can be used in any order you wish.

Below are brief guidance notes for using the CD-ROM. For more detailed information, please click on the '?' button in the top right-hand corner of the screen.

The program contains the following:
- The extract pages from the book.
- All of the photocopiable pages from the book.
- Additional printable pages.
- Interactive on-screen activities.
- Media resources.

Getting started

Put the CD-ROM into your CD-ROM drive. If you do not have a CD-ROM drive, phone Scholastic Customer Services on 0845 6039091.

- For Windows users, the install wizard should autorun, if it fails to do so then navigate to your CD-ROM drive. Then follow the installation process.
- For Mac users, copy the disk image file to your hard drive. After it has finished copying double click it to mount the disk image. Navigate to the mounted disk image and run the installer. After installation the disk image can be unmounted and the DMG can be deleted from the hard drive.
- To install on a network, please see the ReadMe file located on the CD-ROM (navigate to your drive).

To complete the installation of the program you need to open the program and click 'Update' in the pop-up. Please note – this CD-ROM is web-enabled and the content will be downloaded from the internet to your hard-drive to populate the CD-ROM with the relevant resources. This only needs to be done on first use, after this you will be able to use the CD-ROM without an internet connection. If at any point any content is updated, you will receive another pop-up upon start up when there is an internet connection.

Main menu

The main menu is the first screen that appears. Here you can access: terms and conditions, registration links, how to use the CD-ROM and credits. To access a specific book click on the relevant button (NB only titles installed will be available). You can filter by the

drop-down lists if you wish. You can search all resources by clicking 'Search' in the bottom left-hand corner. You can also login and access favourites that you have bookmarked.

Resources

By clicking on a book on the main menu, you are taken to the resources for that title. The resources are: Media, Interactives, Extracts and Printables. Select the category and then launch a resource by clicking the play button.

Teacher settings

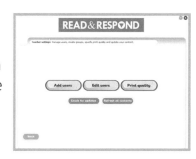

In the top right-hand corner of the screen is a small 'T' icon. This is the teacher settings area. It is password protected, the password is: login. This area will allow you to choose the print quality settings for interactive activities ('Default' or 'Best') and also allow you to check for updates to the program or re-download all content to the disk via Refresh all content. It is from here that you can set up user logins so that you can save and access favourites. Once a user is set up, they can enter by clicking the login link underneath the 'T' and '?' buttons.

Search

You can access an all resources search by clicking the search button on the bottom-left of the main menu. You can search for activities by type (using the drop-down filter) or by keyword by typing into the box. You can then assign resources to your favourites area or launch them directly from the search area.

▼ CURRICULUM LINKS

Section	Activity	Curriculum objectives
Guided reading		Comprehension: To develop positive attitudes to reading and understanding of what they read.
Shared reading	1	Comprehension: To draw inferences such as inferring characters' feelings, thoughts and motives; to use similes and metaphors.
	2	Comprehension: To discuss and evaluate figurative language.
	3	Comprehension: To draw inferences, justifying inferences with evidence.
	4	Comprehension: To retrieve, record and present information from non-fiction.
Grammar, punctuation & spelling	1	Composition: To use the passive voice to affect the presentation of information in a sentence.
	2	Composition: To understand how words are related by meaning as synonyms and antonyms.
	3	Composition: To recognise vocabulary and structures that are appropriate for formal speech and writing.
	4	Composition: To use relative clauses beginning with who, which, where, when, whose, that.
	5	Composition: To link ideas across paragraphs using adverbials.
	6	Composition: To use punctuation to mark independent clauses.
Plot, character & setting	1	Comprehension: To draw inferences, such as inferring characters' feelings, thoughts and motives.
	2	Comprehension: To summarise ideas from more than one paragraph.
	3	Comprehension: To draw inferences such as inferring characters' feelings, thoughts and motives.
	4	Comprehension: To predict what might happen from details stated or implied.
	5	Spoken language: To use spoken language to develop understanding through speculating, hypothesising, and exploring ideas.
	6	Comprehension: To summarise ideas from more than one paragraph.
	7	Comprehension: To summarise ideas from more than one paragraph.
	8	Comprehension: To draw inferences such as inferring characters' feelings, thoughts and motives.

Section	Activity	Curriculum objectives
Talk about it	1	Spoken language: To ask relevant questions to extend understanding.
	2	Spoken language: To participate in role play and improvisations.
	3	Spoken language: To gain, maintain and monitor the listener's interest.
	4	Spoken language: To use spoken language to develop understanding through imagining and exploring ideas.
	5	Spoken language: To consider and evaluate different viewpoints, building on the contributions of others.
	6	Spoken language: To maintain attention and participate actively in collaborative conversations.
Get writing	1	Composition: To describe settings, characters and atmosphere.
	2	Composition: To précis longer passages; to learn conventions of diary writing.
	3	Composition: To identify the purpose of the writing, selecting appropriate form.
	4	Composition: To précis longer passages.
	5	Composition: To identify the purpose of the writing, selecting appropriate form.
	6	Comprehension: To predict what might happen from details stated and implied.
Assessment	1	Composition: To identify the purpose of the writing, selecting appropriate form.
	2	Composition: To use present and past tenses correctly.
	3	Comprehension: To ask questions to improve understanding.
	4	Transcription: To use knowledge of morphology and etymology in spelling.
	5	Transcription: To distinguish between homophones.
	6	Composition: To précis longer passages.

KENSUKE'S KINGDOM

About the book

Michael Morpurgo has said that he always wanted to write a desert-island story – his own favourite stories include *Treasure Island* by Robert Louis Stevenson and *Robinson Crusoe* by Daniel Defoe.

Why the Whales Came (1985) and *The Wreck of the Zanzibar* (1995) both have island themes. The idea for *Kensuke's Kingdom* came when someone sent Morpurgo a newspaper cutting about a Japanese soldier who had survived on a remote island for 40 years after the Second World War. He had also read about a family who sold up everything, bought a yacht and went on a round-the-world voyage.

Encouraged by a request from a young reader for a desert-island story, Morpurgo was finally inspired by the name of a dog – Stella Artois – which belonged to a little girl on a visit to his Farms for City Children project. When Professor Tonimoto from Japan came to interview him about his writing, Morpurgo turned the interview around, researching Japan and the Japanese for the character of Kensuke.

About the author

Michael Morpurgo was born in St Albans in 1943. At school, his favourite subjects were rugby, cricket and geography. He began writing for children when he was a teacher, encouraged by the children's responses to stories he read to them. His first book was published in 1975. He has since had more than 100 books and several screenplays published, and his writing has been translated into 26 different languages. He says he writes for the 'inner child' inside him, writing in an exercise book propped up on pillows on his bed. His stories are often based on real-life events, such as the discovery of a sword, shield and mirror in a farmer's field on the Isles of Scilly, which inspired *The Sleeping Sword*.

Michael Morpurgo lives on a farm in Devon, where he runs Farms for City Children with his wife Clare. He began the project in 1976, to give city children experience of life on a farm, and now has three farms that children can visit. He has won many awards for children's books, including the Smarties Book Prize, the Whitbread Award, and the Children's Book of the Year Award, and has had books adapted for stage and television. He was awarded the MBE in 1999 and the OBE in 2006 and was Children's Laureate from 2003 to 2005.

Key facts

First published: 1999

Illustrator: Michael Foreman

Awards: Winner of the Children's Book Award; Shortlisted for the Whitbread and Federation of Children's Book Awards; Nominated for the Carnegie Medal 2000.

Did you know: It was adapted into a play by Stuart Paterson in 2005.

First reading

Look together at the front cover of *Kensuke's Kingdom*. Ask the children what sort of story they think this will be. (Adventure, exciting, scary.) Ask: *What does the picture convey?* (A sailing boat in danger.) Next, read the back cover blurb. Pick out the words 'a modern day Robinson Crusoe'. Do the children know what this refers to? (*Robinson Crusoe* is an adventure story by Daniel Defoe, in which the central character is marooned on a desert island.) Ask: *What is the main 'hook' in the blurb that makes the reader want to read the story?* (To find out what happens to Michael and who leaves him food.) Look next at the map (facing the title page). Can the children deduce from this what 'Kensuke's Kingdom' refers to? (The island where Michael is marooned.) Note that these questions may need to be adapted depending on which edition of the book you are using.

Chapters 1 and 2

Read the first two paragraphs of Chapter 1 together and ask the children what questions they raise. (How did Michael disappear? How did he come back from the dead? Why has he had to keep his story secret for ten years?) Continue reading to the end of Chapter 1. Ask the children what happens to change Michael's life. (His parents are made redundant; they decide to sail round the world.)

Read to the end of Chapter 2. Ask: *Which two things does Michael find most comforting on the voyage?* (Stella Artois and his football.) What do the children think Michael means when he describes the football as 'a sort of talisman'? (It will bring him luck and keep him safe.) Tell the children to keep in mind question 9 on the bookmark (page 12), and together discuss questions 1 and 2.

Chapters 3 and 4

Read the entries in the log and the short paragraph afterwards ending 'After that it's just empty pages.' Why do the children think Michael's log ends so suddenly? Ask the children to answer

question 7 on the bookmark.

Continue reading for a few more pages until the line ending '...without a care in the world' in Chapter 4. Ask the children to summarise what has happened. How do they think Michael has reached the island? Remind them how he felt the football was his talisman – how has this come true? (It kept him afloat.)

Read until 'We had survived.' Ask: *How is Michael feeling at this point?* Can the children suggest three things he will need to survive on a desert island? (Water, food, shelter.) Together discuss question 12 on the bookmark. Ask the children how long they think someone can survive without food (a few weeks) or without water (just three or four days).

Read to when Michael finds the food left for him (to '...fearful at this revelation or overjoyed.') Ask: *What does Michael's discovery mean?* (He is not alone.) Ask the children to consider question 3 on the bookmark. Read on to the end of Chapter 4. Ask: *What is Michael trying to do?* (Send a smoke signal to boats so he can be rescued.) Ask what the surprise at the end of the chapter is and what we are left wondering. (The man who has helped him is now putting out his fire – why?) Together discuss question 6 on the bookmark.

Chapters 5 and 6

Read Chapter 5 until the line ending '...unless he was out of his head and completely mad.' Ask the children what they have learned about Kensuke so far.

Continue to the end of Chapter 5. Invite the children to list the main problems Michael faces. (Insect bites; sunburn; depending on Kensuke for food and water.) Ask: *How does he feel towards Kensuke and why?* Ask the children to address question 13 on the bookmark.

Read Chapter 6. Ask the children to suggest answers to question 4 on the bookmark. Ask: *Why was Kensuke trying to stop Michael swimming? How does Michael interpret it, and what is the real reason?*

Chapter 7 to the end

Let the children read Chapters 7 and 8. Ask them to summarise what Michael now knows about Kensuke. Ask: *How is he feeling towards him. Why does he feel he has betrayed him?* Ask the children to respond to question 10 on the bookmark.

Read Chapter 9 together and ask the children what helps change Kensuke's mind about Michael's need to go home. (The orang-utan and her baby.) Ask: *What has helped the two of them reach an understanding?* (Dialogue; playing football; working together to help the animals.) Discuss question 8 on the bookmark.

Read on to the end of the story. Ask the children if they think it is a good ending. Why or why not? Would they describe it as happy or sad, or both?

Finish by discussing question 16 on the bookmark.

Second reading

Before reading the book again, ask the children if they think it is likely to be a true story. Ask: *What seems realistic, and what might be fictional?* Ask them if they think that Kensuke is a real character – refer to the letter from his son at the end of the book.

Ask the children what they know about the Second World War (1939–45). Do they have any relatives who remember this time? Give a brief explanation of the causes of the war (Hitler's invasion of neighbouring countries), its dates and the countries that fought against each other (Britain and her Allies, Germany and her Allies). Explain that Japan was an ally of Germany. After Japan bombed American ships at Pearl Harbor in 1941, the Americans entered the war, bringing it to an end in 1945 when they dropped atomic bombs onto the Japanese cities of Nagasaki and Hiroshima.

Tell the children that about a third of the city of Nagasaki was destroyed, and nearly 150,000 people were killed or injured. If possible, use the internet to access and print out reports of Japanese soldiers surviving the war and who were believed to be hiding in jungles on islands in the Philippines decades later. Tell the children the story of Hiroo Onoda, who went into hiding on Lubang for almost 30 years after the Americans took the island in 1944. Explain that Japanese soldiers saw capture or surrender as a kind of dishonour.

Elicit that the writer has invented a fictional story, but that it is based on things that have really happened. Tell the children that Michael Morpurgo was inspired by reading newspaper reports about a family selling their home to sail around the world, and also of a Japanese soldier who lived in hiding on a remote island for decades after the war, not knowing its outcome.

Sailing round the world

Re-read the first two chapters of the book together. Ask the children to identify the initial trigger for the adventure. (The letter Michael's parents receive.) Ask: *What do we learn about Michael at the beginning of the story?* (He is an ordinary boy; enjoys football; has a best friend called Eddie.) Can the children suggest what they would like or dislike about Michael's life on board the *Peggy Sue*?

Read Chapter 3, pausing to look at the pages from Michael's log in the illustration. Ask what sort of dangers and difficulties Michael and his parents have to overcome on their voyage. Establish how this might prepare him for his adventure on the island. (They have to survive hostile weather, a monotonous diet, and so on.)

Marooned!

Look at the illustration at the beginning of Chapter 4. Ask: *How is this chapter a turning point in Michael's adventure?* (He is now alone; the sea journey is over and he has to survive on his own.) Read on, pausing at the description of his rescue, and ask the children if they can recall how Michael has reached the island. Finish the chapter, then ask the children to list all the things that Michael has discovered about the island. (Such as – what the terrain is like; what there is to eat; who or what lives there, and so on.) Ask the children to address question 14 on the bookmark.

Kensuke

Read Chapter 5 and ask the children why the relationship between Michael and Kensuke is so difficult. (They do not share a language.) Ask: *Other than words, in what ways does Kensuke communicate with Michael?* (Gestures; drawing on the sand; bringing him gifts.) Together discuss question 15 on the bookmark.

Continue reading through to the end of Chapter 7. Together, consider question 5 on the bookmark. Ask the children to summarise the main events and how they have changed the relationship between the two main characters. Ask: *What questions still remain unanswered about Kensuke?*

Read Chapter 8. Pause at the beginning and ask the children why they think finding the football is so important for Michael. (It is a link with home and Eddie; it is his talisman.) Ask the children what questions are answered in this chapter for Michael. (How he came to be saved; where Kensuke gets his belongings.) Encourage the children to explain what happens with the Coke bottle. (Stella Artois thought that they were playing fetch; Kensuke feels betrayed.) Ask the children to answer question 11 on the bookmark.

Rescue

Read Chapters 9 and 10. Ask the children to précis the events in Chapter 9. Ask: *What happens when the killer men arrive?* Can the children explain why Kensuke decides to stay on the island in the end? Ask: *How does Michael feel when he sees the boat? What does Kensuke suggest they do to remember each other?* (To think of each other when they see the full moon.)

Read the postscript together. Ask: *What happened that Kensuke did not know about?* (His family was saved because they were on a visit to the grandmother.) Ask the children in what ways they think this adventure changes the life of Michael, Kensuke and Kensuke's family.

SCHOLASTIC
READ&RESPOND
Bringing the best books to life in the classroom

Kensuke's Kingdom
by Michael Morpurgo

Focus on...
Meaning

1. Explain why navigation skills are an important part of Michael's journey. How might it change life for Michael and his parents?

2. How many days do you think they spent at sea? Skim and scan to see if you can work it out.

3. What does Michael's discovery of food and water mean? What questions would he want to ask?

4. Why does Michael charge down the beach and into the sea? What is he feeling when he does this?

5. How many days do you think Michael was ill? Look for clues.

6. Does much time pass before Michael can light a fire? What events occur before he lights one? Why does the author include these events?

Focus on...
Organisation

7. Focus on the ship's log. Explain how it fits into the main narrative. How is it a key part?

8. Look at the illustration at the end of Chapter 9 and beginning of Chapter 10. There are three scenes. Do the scenes join together? What do they tell us?

SCHOLASTIC
READ&RESPOND
Bringing the best books to life in the classroom

Kensuke's Kingdom
by Michael Morpurgo

Focus on...
Language and features

9. Note any examples you find of nautical (sailing) terms.

10. How does the author let us know that Michael feels guilty about sending a message in a bottle?

11. How does the author describe the way Kensuke feels about Michael's note? Find examples.

Focus on...
Purpose, viewpoints and effects

12. When Michael gets to the peak of the hill he realises that he's on an island and begins to make plans. He knows he needs water and food. What else will he need?

13. What are your initial reactions to Kensuke? Why is this?

14. Would you enjoy Michael's life on the island? Why do you say that?

15. Kensuke could speak little English when he lived in London – but he learns quickly from Michael. Why has the author done this?

16. Should Kensuke have left the island with Michael? Think about the reasons for and against this.

Extract 1

- Read an enlarged copy of Extract 1 from Chapter 4. Ask the children what has happened to Michael, and how he is feeling. (Elated to have survived, but realising that he is alone.) Ask them to pick out all the words that describe Michael's emotions about his situation ('apprehension', 'terrifying', 'dreadful', 'comforted', 'elated'). Can they suggest alternative words?

- Encourage the children to summarise the features of the landscape that Michael views from the hilltop (sea; beach; twin peaks; forest).

- Highlight the word 'swathe' and ask the children if they can explain what it means.

- Underline the repetition of the word 'sea' and ask the children what effect it has. (It emphasises that the sea is all around him.)

- Ask the children to find a simile and a metaphor used to describe the island ('shaped like a peanut'; 'a green jewel'). Point to the words 'silken shimmering', and revise alliteration. Ask: *What do the two adjectives suggest about the sea?*

- Tell the children that these features are good examples of the author's use of descriptive language. Invite them to try paring away the descriptive words and phrases leaving just the bare facts; this can be done as a speaking activity. For example, they read aloud the sentence beginning 'There was a long swathe of brilliant white beach...' then reduce this to 'There were beaches on both sides of the island and another hill at the far end.' When they have done this, encourage the children to consider how the visual, descriptive language contributes to the picture of the island in our imagination.

Extract 2

- Read Extract 2 from Chapter 4 with the class. Ask: *What is the focus of this description of the forest?* (Its sounds.) Encourage the children to underline all the nouns formed from present participles that describe sounds ('howling', 'chanting', 'tapping', 'scraping').

- Can the children find any similes and a metaphor? ('a tapping like a woodpecker', 'a grating noise like frogs', 'the whole orchestra')

- Revise alliteration and ask the children to find examples (whirred and whined; scraping, scratching; grunting grating; cackled and croaked).

- Highlight the word 'mellifluous'. Do the children know what it means? Examine the word root, explaining that *mellus* is the Greek word for honey. (*Melli-fluous* = honey flowing or sounding.)

- Look at the sentence beginning 'The jungle droned...'. Elicit that the writer personifies the jungle by making it the subject of the verbs. Discuss in what other context could the verbs 'droned' and 'cackled' be used? (Bees or aeroplanes; people laughing.)

- Encourage the children to attempt to classify the many kinds of sounds under different headings, for example: music ('evensong', 'chanting', 'the whole orchestra'); machinery ('whirred', 'droned'); or voices ('howling', 'croaked'). Ask: *What impact does mixing so many different kinds of sound have?* (It helps to create the impression of an overwhelmingly noisy cacophony.)

- Ask: *Which other sense distracts Michael?* (The memory of how the sausages smelled.) Explain that the sense of smell is closely linked with memory. Encourage the children to cite examples of this from their own memory banks.

Extract 3

- Read Extract 3 from Chapter 5 together. Ask the children to summarise Michael's first impression of Kensuke, listing some key descriptive adjectives ('old', 'thin', 'angry'). Ask: *Why does Stella reacts as she does to Kensuke?* (Stella recognises that Kensuke has brought them food.)

- Encourage the children to underline all the adjectives describing Kensuke. Can they explain the meaning of 'diminutive', 'agitated', 'ancient' and 'skeletal'? Ask them which details emphasise that Kensuke is old. (His hair, his skin.) Ask: *What do the words used to describe his breeches imply?* ('Tattered' – that he has had them a long time; 'bunched at the waist' – that he is thinner than he once was.)

- Ask: *What else can we deduce about Kensuke from this first encounter?* (Although old, he is still fit enough to run fast; he has been living an outdoor life on the island as his skin is copper tanned).

- Ask the children to pick out the verbs that convey Kensuke's emotions ('agitated', 'trembling', 'accusing', 'fury'; 'scuttled', 'gesticulating', 'haranguing'). Ask: *What do these words suggest?* (Anger and fear.)

- Ask: *What might suggest to Michael that Kensuke poses a threat to him?* (The knife, the stick, the angry voice.) *What suggests that he has no need to fear him?* (Stella's reaction to him; the fact that he stops as he reaches Michael; he is out of breath from running.)

- Discover whether the children can translate the Japanese word *'Dameda'*. (Danger.) Ask them to suggest what Kensuke would say to Michael if the two shared a common language.

Extract 4

- Read Extract 4, a non-fiction text about the island of Lubang, with the class. Explain that the island of Lubang is where the Japanese soldier Hiroo Onoda – the inspiration for Kensuke – survived for more than 30 years after the Second World War ended. Ask the children who they think the text is aimed at. (Tourists; people wanting to learn about the terrain or climate of Lubang.)

- Underline any unfamiliar words ('verdant', 'pristine') and ask the children to provide synonyms (lush and green; clean and unspoiled).

- Refer back to Extract 1, inviting the children to compare and contrast Michael's description of the island with this description of the real-life island and its terrain.

- Challenge the children to find similarities between Lubang and the fictional island. (It is hot and verdant; it has unspoiled white beaches; steep slopes; thick forest.) Now focus on the differences. (Michael's island is much smaller and uninhabited.)

- Ask them to highlight features of the island that appear in the novel: the cave where Kensuke has made his home; the forest; the fruit that Kensuke leaves for Michael; the rainstorm, and so on.

- Focus on the style of the extract and invite comments on the difference between a factual text aimed at visitors or researchers and Michael's own personal impressions of the island where he finds himself marooned. The non-fiction text is objective, methodical and comprehensive in recording facts and figures, whereas Michael's description is subjective ('looked perhaps', 'no more'), uses simile ('like a peanut'), metaphor ('a green jewel') and personal detail ('not so high as mine', 'so far as I could see') and repetition for emphasis ('Sea. Sea. Sea').

Extract 1

The sun was blazing down. I had not really felt the burning heat of it until then. I scanned the horizon. If there was a sail somewhere out there in the haze, I could not see it. And then it came to me that even if I were to see a sail, what could I do? I couldn't light a fire. I had no matches. I knew about cavemen rubbing sticks together, but I had never tried it. I looked all round me now. Sea. Sea. Sea. Nothing but sea on all sides. I was on an island. I was alone.

The island looked perhaps two or three miles in length, no more. It was shaped a bit like an elongated peanut, but longer at one end than the other. There was a long swathe of brilliant white beach on both sides of the island, and at the far end another hill, the slopes steeper and more thickly wooded, but not so high as mine. With the exception of these twin peaks the entire island seemed to be covered with forest. So far as I could see there was no sign of any human life. Even then, as I stood there, that first morning, filled with apprehension at the terrifying implications of my dreadful situation, I remember thinking how wonderful it was, a green jewel of an island framed in white, the sea all about it a silken shimmering blue. Strangely, perhaps comforted somehow by the extraordinary beauty of the place, I was not at all down-hearted. On the contrary I felt strangely elated. I was alive. Stella Artois was alive. We had survived.

Extract 2

The howling had started up again far away in the forest, a last mellifluous evensong, a chanting that went on and on until darkness covered the island. Insects (that is what I presumed they were anyway) whirred and whined from the forest. There was hollow tapping, like a frantic woodpecker. There was scraping, scratching, and a grunting grating noise that sounded like frogs. The whole orchestra of the jungle was tuning up. But it wasn't the sounds that frightened me, it was those phantom eyes. I wanted to be as far as possible from those eyes. I found a small cave at one end of the beach with a dry sandy floor. I lay down and tried to sleep, but Stella would not let me. She whined at me in the pain of her hunger and thirst, so that I slept only fitfully.

The jungle droned and cackled and croaked, and all night long the mosquitoes were at me too. They whined in my ears and drove me mad. I held my hands over my ears to shut out the sound of them. I curled myself round Stella, tried to forget where I was, to lose myself in dreams. I remembered then that it was my birthday, and thought of my last birthday back at home with Eddie and Matt, and the barbecue we'd had in the garden, how the sausages had smelled so good. I slept at last.

Extract 3

He was diminutive, no taller than me, and as old a man as I had ever seen. He wore nothing but a pair of tattered breeches bunched at the waist, and there was a large knife in his belt. He was thin, too. In places – under his arms, round his neck and his midriff – his copper brown skin lay in folds about him, almost as if he'd shrunk inside it. What little hair he had on his head and his chin was long and wispy and white.

I could see at once that he was very agitated, his chin trembling, his heavily hooded eyes accusing and angry. '*Dameda*! *Dameda*!' he screeched at me. This whole body was shaking with fury. I backed away as he scuttled up the beach towards me, gesticulating wildly with his stick, and haranguing me as he came. Ancient and skeletal he may have been, but he was moving fast, running almost. '*Dameda*! *Dameda*!' I had no idea what he was saying. It sounded Chinese or Japanese, maybe.

I was about to turn and run when Stella, who, strangely, had not barked at him at all, suddenly left my side and went bounding off towards him. Her hackles were not up. She was not growling. To my astonishment she greeted him like a long lost friend.

He was no more than a few feet away from me when he stopped. We stood looking at each other in silence for a few moments. He was leaning on his stick, trying to catch his breath. 'Americajin? Americajin? American? *Eikokujin*? British?'

'Yes,' I said, relieved to have understood something at last. 'English, I'm English.'

Extract 4

The verdant island of Lubang is the largest in a group of islands that lie north-west of Mindoro in the Philippines. Measuring 25 kilometres long by up to 6.2 kilometres wide, the island covers 125 square kilometres and has a population of around 25,000. The main industries are farming, fishing and tourism. The climate is tropical, being warm and wet all year round with an average temperature of 27°C, and the risk of seasonal cyclones. Much of the island is clothed in thick forest, containing vines, giant ferns and stinging shrubs and trees like the Lipa, which has hairy leaves with stinging cells. Fruit-bearing trees provide jackfruit, cashew nuts, coconuts, guavas, mangoes, bananas and pineapple. The dense canopy is home to a variety of jungle animals, including wild boar, chickens, forest mice, snakes, birds and insects. The terrain is steep and mountainous in places, with deep canyons, waterfalls and clear, meandering streams. Giant slabs, boulders and shallow caves are formed from the local 'black tiger' marble, which displays black and purple stripes when wet. The caves are home to fruit bats and swallows, whose nests are prized in Japan for the delicacy *nido* soup. Visitors can enjoy exploring the pristine white beaches, snorkelling, scuba diving and trekking as well as following the Onoda trail to learn how the Japanese soldier survived for over 30 years in the jungle.

GRAMMAR, PUNCTUATION & SPELLING

1. Switching subjects

Objective
To understand and use the passive voice.

What you need
Copies of *Kensuke's Kingdom*.

What to do

- Write the following pair of sentences on the board.
  - Michael Morpurgo wrote *Kensuke's Kingdom*.
  - *Kensuke's Kingdom* was written by Michael Morpurgo.

- Underline the verbs and use the terms 'active verb' and 'passive verb'. Ask the children to explain how the verb impacts the sentence: the active verb puts the focus on the author; the passive verb on the book. Expand each sentence as follows.
  - Michael Morpurgo wrote *Kensuke's Kingdom*. *Kensuke's Kingdom* is based on a real-life story.
  - *Kensuke's Kingdom* was written by Michael Morpurgo. Michael Morpurgo has written more than 100 children's books.

- Explain that passive verbs are used to introduce someone or something that becomes the subject of the next sentence. Circle Kensuke's Kingdom and Michael Morpurgo in the first sentence of each pair, then circle them again as they act as the subject in each of the following sentences.

- Write on the board: Michael's father bought the *Peggy Sue*. Ask the children to suggest the next sentence, turning the *Peggy Sue* into the subject, for example: Michael's father bought the *Peggy Sue*. The *Peggy Sue* was a 42-foot yacht.

- List the following on the board: Kensuke, Michael, Stella Artois, the jungle.

Differentiation
Support: Write the sentences on the board to make the children more familiar with the sentence pattern.
Extension: Challenge children to write a pair of sentences about each subject, following the same pattern. They should refer to the novel to find content for their sentences.

2. Similar and opposite

Objective
To find and use synonyms and antonyms.

What you need
Copies of *Kensuke's Kingdom*, interactive activity 'Swap and switch'.

Cross-curricular link
Geography

What to do

- First, work through the interactive activity 'Swap and switch' as a class, finding synonyms and antonyms for the underlined words. Use the activity to revise the meaning of 'synonym' and 'antonym'. The children will also be practising spelling skills as they contribute suggestions.

- Read the first paragraph from Chapter 5. Ask the children to identify adjectives and write them on the board ('diminutive', 'thin', 'little', 'long', 'wispy', 'white'). Challenge them, in pairs, to find one or more synonyms and antonyms for each word.

- As a class, list their suggestions under each adjective. Encourage them to spell aloud the words they contribute, and invite others to confirm or correct their spellings.

- Pairs should then find descriptive words and phrases about the island (Chapter 4) such as 'a long swathe of brilliant white beach'. Ask them to write these down and then find synonyms and antonyms for as many of the adjectives as they can. For example, 'a short stretch of dull black/dark beach'. Share their findings as a class.

Differentiation
Support: Work through the list of adjectives describing Kensuke together, listing synonyms and antonyms on the board. Ask them to think of other words describing appearances. Find synonyms and antonyms for each word found.
Extension: Children can work in pairs to find more words describing people or places in the novel, and then suggest synonyms and antonyms for them.

3. Formal or informal?

Objective

To identify and use formal and informal writing.

What you need

Copies of *Kensuke's Kingdom*, printable pages 'My blog' and 'Postcards'.

What to do

- Read together the first three paragraphs of Michael's diary entry for October 11 in Chapter 3. Allow the children to summarise the content. Discuss the style of the writing. Ask: *Is it formal or informal? Why?* (Informal – it is Michael's personal record.)

- List informal text features. (Short or incomplete sentences lacking a subject: 'Saw flying fish…'; informal connectives: 'else'; informal sentence ending: 'maybe'.)

- In pairs, allow children to rehearse a phone call from Michael to Eddie, relating the news for October 11. Consider how Michael would report his experiences, and how Eddie might respond. Prompt deductive thought: when Michael remarks on the hot weather, what might Eddie say about the weather back home in October?

- Invite pairs to perform their dialogue and discuss the speech style in relation to the diary entry.

- The children can draft the same day's news as a postcard to Eddie using the printable page 'Postcards'.

- Pairs can then draft a formal report for a ship's log using the printable page 'My blog'. First, discuss formal style features: longer, complete sentences; technical terms and names; how the log would plot the boat's course.

Differentiation

Support: Focus on the speech activity. Pairs should write a short recount of the day in a simple, factual way before they begin.

Extension: Working in pairs, the children choose another diary entry and formal log to turn into dialogue between Michael and Eddie.

4. It's all relative

Objective

To understand and use relative clauses.

What you need

Copies of *Kensuke's Kingdom*, photocopiable page 22 'It's all relative'.

Cross-curricular link

History

What to do

- On the board, list relative pronouns: which, who, what, where, when, whose, that. Write the words, 'The Second World War…' and challenge the children to extend the sentence using different relative pronouns. For example, 'The Second World War, which began in 1939, ended in 1945.'

- Suggest subjects, such as Kensuke, Michael, the *Peggy Sue*, and again ask the children to extend the sentence using a relative pronoun, such as 'Michael, whose parents bought the *Peggy Sue*, went on a world trip.'

- In pairs, ask children to complete photocopiable page 22 'It's all relative'. When they have finished, ask pairs to read out their sentences. Were there any variations (such as the soldier, 'whose name was' or 'who was lost in the jungle')? Query key spellings as they read ('who's' or 'whose').

- As a class activity, challenge the children to extend their sentences using relative pronouns, or combine clauses from different sentences using relative pronouns. For example, 'The soldier, whose name was Hiroo Onoda, went into hiding in 1944 when the Americans took the island of Lubang.'

Differentiation

Support: Before they begin writing, read the sentences aloud and discuss which relative pronouns may fit: is it a person, a place or a time. Practise some sentences to establish where to insert the relative pronoun and clause.

Extension: The children can write their own sentences containing a relative pronoun using subjects taken from the novel.

5. Links in time and place

Objective

To use adverbials to link paragraphs.

What you need

Copies of *Kensuke's Kingdom*, photocopiable page 23 'Links in time and space'.

What to do

- Can the children remember the day or point in time that Michael disappeared? (The night before his 12th birthday.) Ask: *Why would this be particularly memorable?* (He would be anticipating birthday celebrations with his parents but instead he was to be alone, marooned on the island.) Focus on the word 'before'. Can they think of other words that tell us when something happens, for example: after, during, since, as soon as, while, when. Explain that adverbials tell us about the time, place or manner in which something happens.

- Give examples of different types of adverbial. 'Kensuke was out fishing when he found Michael' (time); 'Kensuke left food for Michael near his cave' (place); 'Kensuke laid out the food neatly' (manner).

- Ask the children to work in pairs to complete photocopiable page 23 'Links in time and space'. The answers are given below. When they have finished, ask volunteers to share their ideas with the class.

- Answers: Stella was up near/by the bow of the boat when the ball went overboard; Michael went overboard when/after the boat veered violently; Kensuke was out fishing when he saw Michael in the water; Kensuke first met Michael after/when he spotted the fire; Kensuke left food for Michael daily/nightly; Michael was marooned for nearly/almost a year.

Differentiation

Support: Provide a list of adverbials for the children to refer to for the photocopiable activity.
Extension: Challenge the children to work with a partner and each think up questions for their partner to answer using an adverbial.

6. List makers

Objective

To use punctuation to divide independent clauses.

What you need

Copies of *Kensuke's Kingdom*, photocopiable page 24 'List makers', interactive activity 'Home from home'.

Cross-curricular link

PSHE

What to do

- Ask the children to think of and write down a list of their favourite things such as music, food, clothes, games. When they have finished, invite volunteers to read out their list, and then discuss different ways to set out lists: using a colon to introduce; bullet points and/or semicolons within lists. Write examples (using their list material, if possible) on the board, such as: My favourite foods: pizza, chocolate, apples, cheese.

- Hand out photocopiable page 24 'List makers' and tell the children to complete it, punctuating their lists correctly using a variety of methods including colons, semicolons and bullet points.

- The children should complete the interactive activity 'Home from home' individually or in pairs. When they have finished, they should make two written lists of the objects Kensuke had found or made, choosing one of the methods of punctuation.

Differentiation

Support: Work through one of the sections on the photocopiable sheet together to establish familiarity with the punctuation.
Extension: Challenge the children to compose more lists using material from the novel, punctuating them correctly.

It's all relative

● Choose a relative pronoun and add a clause to each of the following sentences, using the fact box below to help you.

> who   what   when   where   whose   that   which

The Second World War did not end in Japan until 1946.

_____

The Japanese soldier was found 30 years after the war ended.

_____

The soldier went into hiding in 1944.

_____

Lubang is an island in the Philippines.

_____

The atom bomb was first used on Hiroshima and Nagasaki in August 1945.

_____

_____

Hiroo Onoda only agreed to leave Lubang in 1974.

_____

Fact box

The war in Europe ended in 1945.
The lost soldier's name was Hiroo Onoda.
The soldier lived in hiding for almost 30 years.
The Americans captured the island of Lubang in 1944.
The atom bomb was tested in July 1945.
Onoda's former Commanding Officer flew to the island in 1974.

Links in time and space

● Answer the questions using different adverbials of time, place or manner.

Where was Stella when the ball went overboard?

_____

_____

What made Michael go overboard?

_____

_____

What was Kensuke doing when he saw Michael in the water?

_____

_____

When did Kensuke first meet Michael?

_____

_____

How often did Kensuke leave food for Michael?

_____

_____

How long was Michael marooned on the island?

_____

_____

List makers

● Make lists of the following using bullet points, colons and semicolons to punctuate them correctly.

Things and places Michael sees on his sea voyage	

The food Kensuke leaves for Michael	

Kensuke's painting materials	

Fishing skills Kensuke teaches Michael	

Kensuke's craft skills	

Kensuke's home-made belongings	

PLOT, CHARACTER & SETTING

1. The sea journey

Objective

To draw inferences, such as inferring characters' feelings, thoughts and motives.

What you need

Copies of *Kensuke's Kingdom*, enlarged world map, coloured sticker dots or felt-tipped pen, photocopiable page 29 'The sea journey', interactive activity 'Map the diary'.

Cross-curricular link

Geography

What to do

- Read Chapter 3 together. Using an enlarged map of the world, ask volunteers to plot each stage of the voyage, using the sticker dots or felt-tipped pen. They can refer to the text and illustrations to help them.

- Ask the children to identify on the map the passages where Michael and his family will be at sea for long periods. Ask: *How does Michael feel when the boat is at sea? How does he feel each time they spot land?*

- Now ask them to identify locations that have different sea conditions, for example, stormy or calm.

- Ask the children to complete the interactive activity 'Map the diary' as a shared task, or work in pairs.

- When they have finished, challenge them to find three things that Michael has never seen before, at sea and on land. Write their suggestions on the board. Discuss how they think this journey might prepare Michael for his experience on the island. (Monotonous diet; bad weather, and so on.)

- Hand out photocopiable page 29 'The sea journey' for the children to complete in pairs, referring to the book to help them.

2. Animal characters

Objective

To summarise ideas from more than one paragraph.

What you need

Copies of *Kensuke's Kingdom*, interactive activities 'Orang-utan quiz' and 'Orang-utan newspaper article'.

Cross-curricular link

Citizenship

What to do

- Read Chapter 4 from 'I sat up...' to 'But I couldn't be at all sure I was right.' Ask what difference it makes to Michael when he sees Stella Artois, and why?

- Challenge them to work in pairs and consider the ways in which Stella is important to the plot. Ask: *Why would the story not happen at all without her?* (She causes Michael to fall overboard.) *How else would the plot change without her?* (The Coke bottle.)

- Bring the class together and write on the board the headings 'Plot', 'Character' and 'Setting'. Ask the children to work in pairs and consider how Stella contributes to each of these aspects. Write their suggestions on the board.

- As a shared activity, do the same for the other animals. For example, the orang-utans bring the killer men to the island (plot); they show how Kensuke lives in harmony with the island (character); they add to the noises and creepy atmosphere (setting).

- Allow the children time to find out more about orang-utans and conservation programmes, using books or the internet, before they attempt the interactive activity 'Orang-utan quiz'. They can then use the interactive activity 'Orang-utan newspaper article' to draft an article on orang-utan conservation for a newspaper.

PLOT, CHARACTER & SETTING

3. Points of view

Objective

To draw inferences such as inferring characters' feelings, thoughts and motives.

What you need

Copies of *Kensuke's Kingdom*.

Cross-curricular links

Citizenship, PSHE

What to do

- Read together the beginning of Chapter 5 as far as '...completely mad.'

- Ask the children to explain what Michael is trying to do (be rescued) and how he is feeling – both about what has happened and towards the stranger. Discuss appropriate words, and write suggestions on the board.

- Now ask them to focus on Kensuke. Can the children explain why he is angry and why he has put out the fire? Again, write relevant words and phrases on the board, asking the children to supply reasons for their suggestions. (For example, he feels afraid because he is worried that the killer men will return.)

- Say that this is just one episode where the two characters have different points of view. Can the children think of any others? (For example, the Coke bottle incident.)

- Tell the children to write a diary account, in the first person, from Kensuke's point of view, of the fire incident. First, prompt them to consider how Kensuke might have first noticed the fire, how he feels about Michael, and so on.

Differentiation

Support: Provide a framework to help the children write their account.

Extension: Ask the children to choose another episode from the story and write another diary entry from Kensuke's point of view.

4. Misunderstandings

Objective

To predict what might happen from details stated or implied.

What you need

Copies of *Kensuke's Kingdom*.

Cross-curricular links

Citizenship, PSHE, geography

What to do

- Read Chapter 6 from 'The air was hot and heavy...' to the end of the chapter. Ask the children what the weather is like. (Hot and humid.) Ask: *How does Michael feel?* (Dejected and frustrated.) *How does it make him feel towards Kensuke?* (It reinforces his resentment.)

- Broaden the discussion to how weather can affect both feelings and actions. (Wet weather might be depressing and keep people indoors.)

- Ask the children to consider why Kensuke behaves as he does. (He puts out the fire because he is worried it might lead the killer men to return; he stops Michael swimming because of the jellyfish, which have arrived after the storm.)

- Elicit that Michael goes into the sea mainly owing to a series of misunderstandings.

- Ask: *What is the main barrier between Kensuke and Michael?* (Language.) Encourage the children to recall what happens next in the story. (Michael is stung by the poisonous jellyfish.)

- Invite the children, in pairs, to imagine that Kensuke appears in time to prevent Michael from entering the sea. Ask: *What might he say, if he could speak English, to persuade Michael that his intentions are well meant? What might Michael reply?*

Differentiation

Support: Work as a whole class to discuss what Michael and Kensuke might say to each other.

Extension: Ask children to write their ideas as a short dialogue between Michael and Kensuke.

5. Counting the days

Objective

To use spoken language to develop understanding through speculating, hypothesising, and exploring ideas.

What you need

Copies of *Kensuke's Kingdom*, photocopiable page 30 'Counting the days'.

What to do

- Ask the children how much time passes in the story. (Almost a year.) Can they cite evidence of this? (Michael says so at the end of the story.) Looking at the ship's log (Chapter 3), can the children work out how long Michael was sailing before that?

- Encourage them to consider how long Kensuke has been on the island.

- Ask them to suggest events that happen quickly, or when the pace quickens. (For example, when Michael is swept overboard.) Write their suggestions on the board.

- Invite them to think about events that happen slowly. (For example, when Michael is waiting to light the beacon.) List these ideas on the board.

- Read Chapter 6 from 'The weather stayed heavy and humid…' to '…my beacon ready and waiting.' Ask the children to find all the words and phrases that suggest time is passing. ('With every day that passed', and so on.)

- Then, read the jellyfish episode in Chapter 6 (from 'I saw him then…'). Ask: *Which words or phrases indicate that this all happens quickly?* ('Suddenly', 'the moment', 'immediate'.)

- Hand out photocopiable page 30 'Counting the days' for the children to complete independently.

Differentiation

Support: Let the children list the main events that happen while Michael is on the island.
Extension: Ask the children to create a timeline of Michael's year on the island, marking in the main events.

6. Picture it!

Objective

To summarise ideas from more than one paragraph.

What you need

Copies of *Kensuke's Kingdom*, drawing materials.

Cross-curricular link

Art and design

What to do

- Read the passage in Chapter 8 together from 'Then one day I need big fish to smoke…' to 'I draw line in sand.' Ask the children to summarise how Kensuke rescues Michael.

- Ask them to recall what Michael remembers of the rescue. Ask: *What saved him from drowning?* (The football.) *Who did he think was rescuing him?* (His parents.)

- Tell the children to imagine they are planning to film the rescue scene for a movie. Explain that film-makers often make storyboards before filming – a sequence of pictures showing how the action develops.

- Let the children re-read Kensuke's version of the rescue, then Michael's account in Chapter 4. Encourage them to decide which scenes they are going to illustrate for their storyboard.

- In their pairs, ask the children to list six scenes, then write brief notes on what each scene should picture.

- Bring the class back together and write their suggestions on the board. Discuss some of the detail that each scene could show, for example, high waves, Michael clinging to the football.

- Let the children draw out the storyboards they have briefed.

Differentiation

Support: Model one scene before they begin.
Extension: Ask the children to write direct speech for each character for every scene.

PLOT, CHARACTER & SETTING

7. Turning points

Objective
To summarise ideas from more than one paragraph.

What you need
Copies of *Kensuke's Kingdom*, interactive activity 'Turning points'.

Cross-curricular link
PSHE

What to do

- Read Chapter 8 from 'But I had another family too.' to the end of the chapter.

- Encourage the children to précis the episode with the Coke bottle. Ask: *Why is Michael torn about sending a message? Why is Kensuke upset?*

- Ask the children what might have occurred if the bottle had reached a finder. Ask: *What happens to prevent this?* (Stella brings it back.) *How does this incident affect the relationship between Michael and Kensuke?*

- Consider together how this event is a turning point: Kensuke realises that Michael really does want to leave the island. Can the children think of other turning points in the story – episodes that change the course of events? (For example, Michael's parents receiving the letter.) Ask them to work in pairs and scan through the text to find examples.

- As a whole class, identify the main episodes that drive the plot forward. (For example, Michael falling overboard.) Discuss what causes each event, and which events happen by accident.

- Ask the children to complete the interactive activity 'Turning points' individually.

Differentiation

Support: Encourage the children to write a bulleted list of the main episodes that drive the plot forward.
Extension: Ask the children to draw a flow chart showing how the main events in the plot are linked.

8. A portrait

Objective
To draw inferences such as inferring characters' feelings, thoughts and motives.

What you need
Copies of *Kensuke's Kingdom*, photocopiable page 31 'A portrait'.

Cross-curricular link
Art and design

What to do

- Write the following headings on the board: 'Action', 'Dialogue' and 'Description'. Ask the children to consider how each contributes to the portrait of Kensuke. *Ask: Which are most important in the first half of the story* (action, description) *and which in the second half* (dialogue)?

- Ask the children to work in pairs to find examples of actions that reveal something about Kensuke's character. List their suggestions on the board.

- Now, encourage the pairs to focus on description and to find examples of Kensuke or his home that describe his character. Ask: *What does Michael mistake him for?* (An orang-utan.) *How does his home reflect his character?* (It is tidy; it shows his skills.) Again, write their suggestions under the appropriate heading on the board.

- Ask the children if they can identify the turning point that leads to more dialogue between Kensuke and Michael. (His sickness.) Ask: *What aspects of Kensuke's character are shown once he is able to communicate with Michael?* (His family; his history.)

- Hand out photocopiable page 31 'A portrait' for the children to complete independently.

Differentiation

Support: Ask the children to draw and label a picture of Kensuke.
Extension: Let the children design a concept map for Kensuke's character, using headings such as 'Appearance', 'Skills' and 'Family'.

The sea journey

● List all the animals that Michael sees on his voyage.

On land	At sea

● List the places he visits.

● Record three stages of the journey when sea conditions were different.

Place	Sea conditions
1	
2	
3	

Counting the days

- Write events from the story that happen over a few minutes.

_____

_____

_____

_____

_____

- Write events from the story that happen over days.

_____

_____

_____

_____

_____

_____

- Write events from the story that happen over weeks or months.

_____

_____

_____

_____

_____

_____

A portrait

- Describe Kensuke's appearance and clothes.

- Record three things Kensuke does and explain what they tell us about him.

Action	What it tells us

- Write three emotions that Kensuke shows in the story, and explain the reasons behind them.

Emotion	Reason behind it

TALK ABOUT IT

1. How it all starts

Objective

To ask relevant questions to extend understanding.

What you need

Copies of *Kensuke's Kingdom*.

What to do

- Read the first two paragraphs of *Kensuke's Kingdom* together. Focus on the dramatic first sentence. Ask what this sentence might suggest. (Michael was lost or kidnapped.) Ask: *What other questions do the first paragraphs raise?* (Who is Kensuke? Why must Michael wait for ten years?)

- Ask: *Why is there a break after the first two paragraphs?* (The story then goes into flashback.) *What do the first two paragraphs establish about Michael's adventure?* (He survives; he became friends with Kensuke.)

- Now read on and finish Chapter 1. Encourage the children, working in pairs, to summarise everything the chapter reveals about Michael.

- As a class, discuss their findings. Ask the children which facts are especially relevant and list these on the board. (The family's love of sailing; Stella Artois.)

- Ask: *What changes the family's life?* (The redundancy letter.) *What else changes?* (They stop sailing; Eddie moves away; the Mudlarks disband.) How do they think Michael is feeling at the end of Chapter 1? (For example, excitement, fear, anticipation.)

- Discuss what the reader wants to find out by the end of this chapter. (What happens; why Michael disappears.) Suggest that these are 'hooks' to keep the reader reading.

Differentiation

Support: Put children in groups of four when summarising the chapter to help generate ideas.
Extension: Ask small groups to discuss the benefits and disadvantages of giving up everyday life and going on an adventure like Michael.

2. A dramatic farewell

Objective

To participate in role play and improvisations.

What you need

Copies *of Kensuke's Kingdom*.

Cross-curricular link

Drama

What to do

- Re-read Chapter 1 at pace. Tell the children they are going to prepare a short radio drama of the farewell scene.

- As a shared activity, ask the children to identify all the characters and write these on the board. Discuss each character, and what we know about them from the text.

- Ask the children to work in small groups to discuss what each character might say in the scene. Encourage them to think about stage directions that would help show how the characters are feeling. (Gran might cry; Barnacle Bill might sound a bit gruff and strict.)

- When they have finished, recap that this is a scene for a radio play. Ask the groups to discuss how to evoke the location through sound effects such as the sound of boat masts, seagulls, the sea, a dog barking.

- Discuss ideas, as a whole class, and write suggestions on the board.

- Ask the groups to prepare a short drama. Each child should take the part of one of the characters. Finally, invite the groups to perform their scenes to the rest of the class.

3. Desert-island skills

Objective

To gain, maintain and monitor the listener's interest.

What you need

Copies of *Kensuke's Kingdom*, photocopiable page 35 'Desert-island skills', interactive activity 'Island foods', printable page 'Fruits of the Tropics', media resource 'Breadfruit'.

What to do

• Begin the lesson by working through the interactive activity 'Island foods' as a shared activity.

• In pairs, ask the children to complete photocopiable page 35, which explores the things Michael and Kensuke used to survive.

• Display media resource 'Breadfruit' and provide children with printable page 'Fruits of the Tropics'. Allow them time to find out some facts about the breadfruit before completing the page. When they have finished, tell the children they are going to use the information they have gathered to prepare a short presentation on breadfruit.

• Allocate them different roles and audiences. For example, they could be a chef talking to a group of trainee cooks; a grower trying to persuade a supermarket buyer to stock breadfruit; or the presenter of a travel or educational programme for radio or television. Encourage them to focus on the information that will be of most interest to their purpose or audience and the style that their speaker might adopt (such as persuasive or factual).

• The printable page can be used as a writing frame for the children to research and make notes on other tropical fruits if time allows.

Differentiation

Support: Provide specific websites or books for the children to find information about breadfruits.

Extension: Let children work use ICT skills to make a video of their presentation.

4. Songs and signs

Objective

To use spoken language to develop understanding through imaging and exploring ideas.

What you need

Copies of *Kensuke's Kingdom*, photocopiable page 36 'Songs and signs', scissors, paper, glue, media resource 'Fingerspelling'.

What to do

• Read together Chapter 7 from 'In all this time...' to 'I resigned myself to waiting.' Challenge the children, in pairs, to list the ways Michael tries to communicate with Kensuke before they can speak. (Smiles; nods; signs; pointing; drawing in the sand.)

• Discuss ways of communicating without words, introducing the concepts of sign language for the deaf, and fingerspelling. Display media resource 'Fingerspelling'. In pairs, ask them to spell the name of a character from the book, then to spell their friend's name using their fingers.

• Ask how difficult they found the task, and how long it might take to learn fingerspelling. Have they tried communicating with people who speak a different language? Explain how different cultures have different customs of greeting (such as bowing, handshaking). Ask: *Which Japanese custom do Kensuke and Michael adopt at the end of each day?* (Bowing to each other.) *How else do they communicate their thoughts in the story?* List their suggestions on the board.

• Hand out photocopiable page 36 for children to complete with their partner. Discuss as a class how each method of communication affects the relationship between Michael and Kensuke. (For example, the message in a bottle is seen as a betrayal.)

Differentiation

Support: Ask the children to sign their own name rather than their friends.

Extension: Challenge the children to sign a sentence to their friend.

5. A big adventure

Objective

To consider and evaluate different viewpoints, building on the contributions.

What you need

Copies of *Kensuke's Kingdom*, media resource 'Tropical island'.

Cross-curricular links

History, geography

What to do

- Discuss with the children what sort of story *Kensuke's Kingdom* is. (Adventure.) Use the media resource 'Tropical island' as a stimulus for thinking of other stories about someone being marooned. (*Robinson Crusoe.*) Challenge them to identify the main features these stories share. (For example, a central character and their story of survival after going overboard.)

- Ask the children to suggest the main features a good adventure story needs. (A fast-moving plot; exotic setting; suspense; a sympathetic character, and so on.) Write their suggestions on the board. Challenge them to work in pairs to find and list examples of each in the story.

- Bring the class together and share their findings. Talk about which elements of *Kensuke's Kingdom* are based on real events (a Japanese soldier living in hiding; men killing orang-utans; a family sailing around the world). Ask: *Does anything happen that is more like fiction than reality?* (The dog gets rescued as well as Michael; the *Peggy Sue* somehow manages to find the island that Michael is living on.) Do they think the writer has made the story credible and, if so, how? Encourage volunteers to present different points of view and use persuasive language to convince others to agree with them.

6. Changes

Objective

To maintain attention and participate actively in collaborative conversations.

What you need

Copies of *Kensuke's Kingdom*, photocopiable page 37 'Changes'.

Cross-curricular links

History, citizenship

What to do

- Read Chapter 9 from 'At every opportunity now...' to '...Kensuke was really serious about it.'

- Ask the children how long they think Kensuke has been on the island. Remind them that Michael arrived on the island in 1988. How much do they think the world had changed since the Second World War ended in 1945? Prompt their suggestions by writing some headings on the board: 'Transport and travel', 'Cities', 'Technology' and 'Environment'.

- Ask the children to work in groups of up to six to discuss what they would tell Kensuke about the way the world has changed if they met him now. The children should include bad as well as good aspects. Share ideas as a class.

- Focus on technology and inventions. Point out that Michael knows of Japan mainly through global brands. Are there any other things the children know about Japan? Ask: *What else might Kensuke ask Michael?*

- Hand out photocopiable page 37 'Changes' and ask the children to fill it in independently.

Differentiation

Support: Ask the children to concentrate on the first two questions only.

Extension: Let groups of up to six imagine they have been marooned for 40 years from now and discuss how the world might change.

Desert-island skills

- Write some of the things that Michael finds for himself on the island.

- Write some of the things that Kensuke provides for Michael.

- Write some of the things Kensuke uses from the shipwreck.

- Write some of the things Kensuke uses on the island and how he uses them.

Resource	How Kensuke uses it

Songs and signs

● Explain how each method of communication is used in the story. When you have finished, cut and paste the boxes in the order that they appear.

The song 'Ten Green Bottles'

A beacon

Gifts

Writing on a rock

A message in a bottle

Changes

● Write down some of the ways these have changed in the last 40 years.

Cities

Homes

Schools

● Write down three things you would tell Kensuke about the world today.

Good things	Bad things
1	
2	
3	

● If Michael stayed on the island for 40 years what changes might he see when he got home?

_____

_____

_____

▼ GET WRITING

1. Get lost!

Objective
To write an example of descriptive, expressive language, based on those read.

What you need
Copies of *Kensuke's Kingdom*.

Cross-curricular link
Art and design

What to do
- Read together Chapter 4 from 'When the beach petered out...' to '...and there was the sea again.' Ask the children what sort of mood is created here.

- Working together, write words from the text like 'impenetrable', 'dark', 'menacing', 'sinister' and 'surreptitious' on the board. Can the children explain what each word means?

- Ask: *What makes Michael feel afraid?* (He feels he is being watched.)

- Focus on the description of sounds, and write nouns like 'shiver', 'cracking', 'rustlings' on the board. What do the children think is causing them? (The orang-utans and gibbons.) Ask: *Why would it be scary for Michael?* (He does not know who else is on the island.) *How does the writer increase suspense?* (The noises come ever closer.)

- Tell the children they are going to imagine they get lost in the forest and write a description of how it feels when they cannot find a way out. Remind them that they should use different senses and describe sounds, the feel of things and smells, as well as things they see. They can then write a paragraph or two of description, in the first person. Share some of the children's paragraphs.

Differentiation
Support: Ask the children to draw a jungle scene, and to write descriptive labels for its main features.
Extension: Encourage the children to write a short description of the jungle in heavy rain, paying attention to sounds as well as sights.

2. Dear diary

Objective
To understand how settings influence events and incidents in stories and how they affect characters' behaviour.

What you need
Copies of *Kensuke's Kingdom*.

Cross-curricular link
Geography

What to do
- Read together Chapter 7 from 'Our life together...' to '...and leave me to mine.'

- Ask the children how they think Michael is feeling about the island at this point. Can they cite any episodes where he feels differently about the island or the jungle? (When it rains; when the jungle is noisy and the insects are biting.) Ask: *What is now different from when he first arrived on the island?* (He has regular meals; sleeps on a mat; has painting as a pastime.)

- Invite the children to work in pairs to map out a page of Michael's diary. They should first write headings suggested in the text (such as 'Breakfast', 'Morning', 'Lunch', and so on), then write notes under each heading, referring to information from the passage.

- When they have finished, ask them to work in their pairs again and use the same headings to write notes for another day in a diary from Michael's old life, before his family went off on their round-the-world trip. They should refer back to the first chapter for information and they can also use their imaginations.

Differentiation
Support: In mixed-ability pairs encourage the children to create notes for the diary entry.
Extension: Let the children work individually and write up a page from Michael's diary using their notes.

3. Art lesson

Objective

To write another text form (instructions) based on knowledge of a story.

What you need

Copies of *Kensuke's Kingdom*, photocopiable page 41 'Art lesson', interactive activity 'Raw materials'.

Cross-curricular link

Art and design

What to do

- Read Chapter 7 together. Ask the children to summarise all the things revealed here about Kensuke's painting. (The tools he uses; the subjects he paints, and so on.) Ask: *Why does he wash away his paintings?* (He is trying to improve his skills.) Discuss as a class how painting on a shell would be different from painting on paper. (Its shape; curves; surface texture.)

- Ask the children to write all the things Michael sees in the cave that relate to Kensuke's painting. Then ask them to list all the things that Kensuke makes to use or eat. (For example, he bottles fruit; he makes spears.)

- Hand out photocopiable page 41 'Art Lesson' for the children to complete independently.

- Challenge the children to complete the interactive activity 'Raw materials'.

- Afterwards, ask the children to write instructions for a lesson in shell painting. Recap the key features of instruction texts (second-person or imperative verbs; division into paragraphs – what you need, method, and so on.)

Differentiation

Support: Ask the children to complete the interactive activity in pairs.

Extension: Ask the children to make an inventory of Kensuke's cave home, dividing items into local materials and things brought from the shipwreck.

4. Happenings

Objective

To write a summary of a book or part of a book.

What you need

Copies of *Kensuke's Kingdom*.

Cross-curricular link

History

What to do

- Read the last chapter together. Ask the children to pick out the main events that happen. Write their suggestions on the board.

- Ask the children how much time they think passes during this chapter. (Days or weeks?) Encourage them to support their answers with evidence from the text.

- Organise the children to work in pairs to construct a timeline showing the main events and the order in which they occur.

- Bring the class back together and as a shared activity, try writing a précis of the chapter in about 100 words. Encourage the children to focus only on the main events (such as the arrival of the junk; the discovery of the dead gibbons) for their summary.

- When they have finished the summary, discuss with the children which events in this chapter have happened before, earlier in the story. (For example, Michael lighting a beacon; the junk coming to the island; the rainy weather.) Ask: *Which things are new events?* (For example, the arrival of the *Peggy Sue*.)

Differentiation

Support: Encourage them to write a bulleted list before proceeding to write their précis.

Extension: Ask the children to précis the main events in the story concerned with Michael's beacon. They should refer to the text to help them find episodes.

5. A letter

Objective

To write a portrait of a character, in a letter.

What you need

Copies of *Kensuke's Kingdom*, photocopiable page 42 'A letter'.

Cross-curricular link

History

What to do

- Read the first paragraph of *Kensuke's Kingdom* together, and then the postscript. Ask the children why Kensuke makes Michael promise to keep quiet for ten years. (He does not want to be found.) Ask: *What does the reader learn from the letter from Kensuke's son?* (He and his mother survived the bombing of Nagasaki.)

- Tell the children that they are going to imagine they are writing a letter from Michael to Michiya about his father. First, they should work in pairs to list the things they think Michiya might want to know. Share ideas as a class.

- Hand out photocopiable page 42 'A letter' to help the children plan their letter. They can work in pairs and refer to the text, but they will need to summarise relevant material. Discuss if there is anything they would exclude from their letter. (For example, how thin and frail Kensuke was.) When they have finished, bring the class back together to discuss their findings.

- Ask the children to use their plan and work individually to write their letter. You will need to invent an address.

Differentiation

Support: Revise the correct layout for a letter.
Extension: Ask the children to use their material to write a dialogue between Michael and Michiya.

6. Kensuke's return

Objective

To write an alternative ending.

What you need

Copies of *Kensuke's Kingdom*, photocopiable page 43 'Kensuke's return', media resource 'Return to Nagasaki'.

Cross-curricular links

Geography, history

What to do

- Read the last chapter together. Discuss Kensuke's reasons for staying on the island. Ask: *How does he feel at the end of the story? How does Michael feel?* Do they think it is a satisfactory conclusion?

- Ask if they can imagine a different ending. Write their suggestions on the board. (Michael might stay, if his parents do not find him; Kensuke might return to Japan.)

- Tell them they are going to plan out an alternative ending, in which Kensuke decides to go home. Remind them that this happened to the real-life character Hiroo Onoda, who had been on an island in the Philippines for 30 years when he returned to Japan. How do they think Kensuke would feel when he got home? Ask: *How would Nagasaki seem to him? What would make him happy or sad?*

- Display media resource 'Return to Nagasaki' and ask them what Kensuke might think when he sees what has happened in Nagasaki while he has been on the island.

- Hand out photocopiable page 43 'Kensuke's return' and tell the children to fill it in.

- Bring the class back together and discuss their ideas.

Differentiation

Support: Provide prompt questions to help the children structure their ideas. For example, ask: *Who will be waiting for him?*
Extension: Ask the children to write an episode from their alternative ending.

Art lesson

- Write all the things from the island that Kensuke uses for painting and explain how he uses them.

Resource	How it is used

- Write step-by-step instructions for making his paint brushes.

1	
2	
3	
4	

- Write some of the subjects that Michael and Kensuke paint on the island.

_____

_____

_____

_____

- Write some subjects they paint from memory.

_____

_____

_____

_____

A letter

- Explain how Kensuke came to be on the island.

_____

_____

_____

_____

- Describe his daily life on the island.

_____

_____

_____

_____

- What does he say about his family and his feelings for them?

_____

_____

_____

_____

- Explain why he decides to remain on the island.

_____

_____

_____

_____

Kensuke's return

- Plan an alternative ending for the story.

What does Michael say to Kensuke to persuade him to go home?

What does Kensuke say to Michael to explain why he has decided to return home?

How does Kensuke get home?

What happens when he arrives home and who greets him?

How does he feel?

How do Kensuke and Michael stay in touch?

ASSESSMENT

1. Letters and narrative

What to do

- Challenge the children to think of some of the ways letters and messages feature in the story. Write their suggestions on the board. (For example, the message that Michael writes to his food benefactor; his message in a bottle; the letter from Kensuke's son in the postscript.) Working in pairs, ask them to work through the novel, making a note of all the letters or messages that are referred to (see Chapters 1, 4, 8; postscript).

- The children should then work individually to complete printable page 'Letters'.

- Discuss the children's findings and extend the discussion to include the motives or emotions surrounding the letters or messages. Ask: *How would Michael's father have felt when he received the letter from the brickworks? What emotions was Michael feeling when he wrote the message in the sand and the message in the bottle? Which of the messages or letters drive the plot?* (For example, when his father is made redundant, it begins the chain of events that leads to Michael being marooned on the island.)

- As a shared class activity, work through the interactive activity 'Chain of events' to help stimulate ideas.

2. Tense questions

What to do

- Write on the board: 'Story narrative', 'Michael's journal', 'Speech/dialogue'. Using these headings, discuss how different tenses are used, and why. In the main narrative, Michael recounts events in the past tense; some of his journal entries use the past, but he uses the present tense when he is describing something as it happens. Kensuke uses the present tense because his English is not perfect.

- Focus on Kensuke's speech explaining how he rescued Michael and Stella (Chapter 8). Discuss how using the present tense conveys that Kensuke is not speaking his native language. Ask the children, in pairs, to correct Kensuke's English by reading aloud his dialogue, replacing present tense with past-tense verbs.

- Next, ask them to choose two paragraphs from the book and experiment by changing one from past to present and one from present to past. Ask volunteers to read out their results. Discuss how altering the tense changes the meaning or effect of the text, identifying the properties of each tense: the present gives immediacy; the past a sense of history. Discuss the 'historic present' and ask if is it more effective for recount than the past tense. For example, 'Michael tried to escape but felt guilty' (past tense) or 'Michael tries to escape but feels guilty' (historic present).

3. True or false?

Objective

To ask questions to improve understanding.

What you need

Copies of *Kensuke's Kingdom*, interactive activity 'Kensuke's quiz'.

Cross-curricular links

History, geography, PSHE, art and design

What to do

- Explain to the children that they are going to work in groups of up to six, to compile questions for a quiz about the novel. They should ask questions that can be answered with either 'True' or 'False'. Provide a model on the board, for example: 'Michael goes overboard when he is 12 years old.' (Answer: False. It is the eve of his twelfth birthday.)'

- Allocate different quiz topics to each group:
  - history (all the facts about Kensuke or the war)
  - geography (all the facts about the island and its terrain)
  - PSHE (all the facts to do with the emotions or feelings the characters experience)
  - art/crafts (all the facts to do with the crafts Kensuke practises and teaches Michael).

- Give the groups time to compile and write five quiz questions. When they have all finished, circulate the quiz questions to other groups, challenging them to answer the questions their classmates have devised under different topics.

- Share answers, encouraging the children to support their answers with evidence from the novel.

- Finish the lesson by completing the interactive activity 'Kensuke's quiz', and use it as a model to compile some of their own multiple-choice questions about the novel.

Differentiation

Support: Provide groups with two or three model questions for their topic.
Extension: The groups can extend their quiz by adding questions for their own or another topic.

4. Spelling bee

Objective

To investigate spelling and understand that the meaning of some words needs to be learned specifically.

What you need

Copies of *Kensuke's Kingdom*.

What to do

- As a class, discuss possible categories for a spelling bee based on words in the novel. For example, words based on: character or setting; a topic such as sailing or orang-utans; words categorised by part of speech. Write their suggestions as headings on the board.

- Allocate groups of up to six one category for the spelling bee. Explain that they need to search the novel for words for a spelling bee. They should try to find difficult or challenging words in that category. For example, the sailing topic could include spellings such as 'Yachtmaster' and 'Bowman'.

- Allow groups time to compile lists of ten words.

- The groups can then compete against each other in the spelling bee. They should take turns to read out words from their lists (nominating a different speaker each time). The other group should confer among themselves before writing down the correct spelling.

- Award points for the group with the most correct spellings and invite suggestions about which words were the hardest to spell.

Differentiation

Support: Provide specific pages for children to find words from the novel to choose for their group category.
Extension: Challenge groups to use a thesaurus to find words with the same or a similar meaning to replace the words on their list for the spelling bee. If there is time, they can use the new lists for another spelling bee.

5. Word search

Objective

To identify and use homophones.

What you need

Copies of *Kensuke's Kingdom*, photocopiable page 47 'Sounds familiar', interactive activity 'Same sounds'.

What to do

- Read the passage in Chapter 6 from 'I sat there…' as far as '…when I like.'

- Ask the children to find a word that has two meanings ('junk') and define them. (A Chinese boat with a flat base; old or worthless things.) Can they compose short sentences using both meanings of the word and suggest what reveals which meaning is intended? (When it refers to the boat, it is used with the indefinite or definite article: 'The junk went out of sight'. For rubbish, it is used as a collective or non-countable noun without an article: 'There was nothing but junk in the shed'.)

- Revise homophones. Ask the children, in pairs, to find homophones for four words in the passage (bear, bare; beach, beech; hear, here; sea, see). Challenge them to compose pairs of short sentences using each homophone correctly. Invite volunteers to read out their sentences.

- Encourage them to see the novel as a rich resource for new words and spellings. Ask them, in pairs, to complete photocopiable page 47. The homophones they should identify are as follows. 1: piece/peace; sun/son; 2: through/threw; I/eye; saw/sore; 3: I/eye; to/too/two; cache/cash; 4: I/eye; steal/steel; 5: hairs/hares; 6: I/eye; to/too/two; 7: one/won; hole/whole.

- Children can also complete the interactive activity 'Same sounds' to practise finding homophones.

Differentiation

Support: Revise homophones by writing pairs of words on the board before they begin the task.
Extension: Challenge learners to find another passage in the book where they can identify homophones and use them to write short sentences.

6. Review

Objective

To write summaries of books or parts of books, deciding priorities relevant to word purpose.

What you need

Printable page 'Review'.

What to do

- Ask the children if they enjoyed *Kensuke's Kingdom* and to explain why or why not.

- Discuss together the story as an example of the adventure genre. Revise some of the key ingredients that make it an adventure story. (For example, an exciting journey; a character who has to face danger alone; an exotic or dramatic setting; a fast-moving plot with surprises and cliffhangers – events that make the reader want to read on to find out what happens next.)

- Ask the children to nominate their favourite parts of the story. Which parts do they find most exciting or scary? Which are sad or moving? Encourage them to give reasons for their answers.

- What do the children think are the writer's main themes in the story? (For example, friendship; survival; a journey – physical and personal; living in harmony with nature.) Ask if they think the story has a satisfactory ending and to give their reasons. Do they find it credible that Michael's parents find him? Ask: *How might the story end otherwise?*

- Encourage the children to work on their own to complete printable page 'Review' using their knowledge of *Kensuke's Kingdom*. Provide separate paper where necessary. When they have finished, discuss their findings.

Sounds familiar

● Find as many homophones as you can in these phrases and sentences from the novel. Write short sentences using all of the homophones you have found to bring out their meaning.

1. A piece of paper, a bit of glass and the sun.

_____

_____

2. Then, through the smoke, I saw him.

_____

_____

3. I began to collect a fresh cache of dry leaves.

_____

_____

4. I could steal the boat.

_____

_____

5. He was trimming hairs with his knife.

_____

_____

6. But I had another family too.

_____

_____

7. One of them was on its back at the bottom of the hole.

_____

_____

SCHOLASTIC

Available in this series:

9781407142203

9781407142197

9781407142241

9781407142227

9781407142234

9781407158754 **JAN 2016**

9781407142258 **JAN 2016**

9781407158778 **JAN 2016**

9781407142289 **JAN 2016**

9781407142319 **JAN 2016**

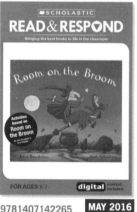

9781407142265 **MAY 2016**

9781407142272 **MAY 2016**

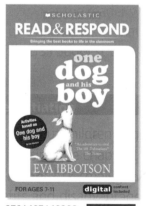

9781407142302 **MAY 2016**

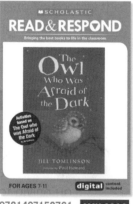

9781407158761 **MAY 2016**

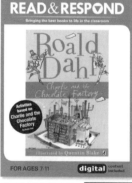

9781407158792 **MAY 2016**

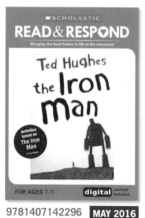

9781407142296 **MAY 2016**

To find out more, call: 0845 6039091
or visit our website www.scholastic.co.uk/readandrespond